W9-CKK-128

Chinese Writing

AN INTRODUCTION

Chinese Writing

AN INTRODUCTION

by Diane Wolff

Calligraphy by Jeanette Chien

Photographs: Collection of C. C. Wang

Holt, Rinehart & Winston
New York

ISBN 0-03-013006-9
Printed in the United States of America
Designer: Joseph Bourke Del Valle

Library of Congress Cataloging in Publication Data

Wolff, Diane.   Chinese writing.

SUMMARY: An introduction to the characteristics of written
and spoken Chinese with a discussion of calligraphy and
instructions for writing characters.
1.   Chinese language—Writing—Juvenile literature.
[1.   Chinese language—Writing]   I.   Chien, Jeanette,
ill.   II.   DeCoppet, Laura, ill.   III.   Larrain, Gilles,
ill.   IV.   McEvoy, Michael, ill.   V.   Title.
PL 1171.W668   495.1′1′1
hc.   ISBN 0-03-013006-9   74-20579   10 9 8 7 6 5 4 3 2
pbk.   ISBN 0-03-048946-6   79-11938   10 9 8 7 6 5 4 3 2 1

For two painters, C. C. Wang and Gerald Johnson

CREDITS

Map by Heidi Palmer
Photographs of masterpieces of calligraphy and art objects
courtesy C. C. Wang
All calligraphy which appears as illustration in text and all dictionary
calligraphy by Jeanette Chien
Handscroll Calligraphy pp. 20, 25 by C. C. Wang
Laura DeCoppet pp. 20, 27(left), 29, 33
Gilles Larrain pp. 27(right), 28(right), 31, 32
Michael McEvoy pp. 25, 26, 28(left)

Contents

Chinese Writing

AN INTRODUCTION

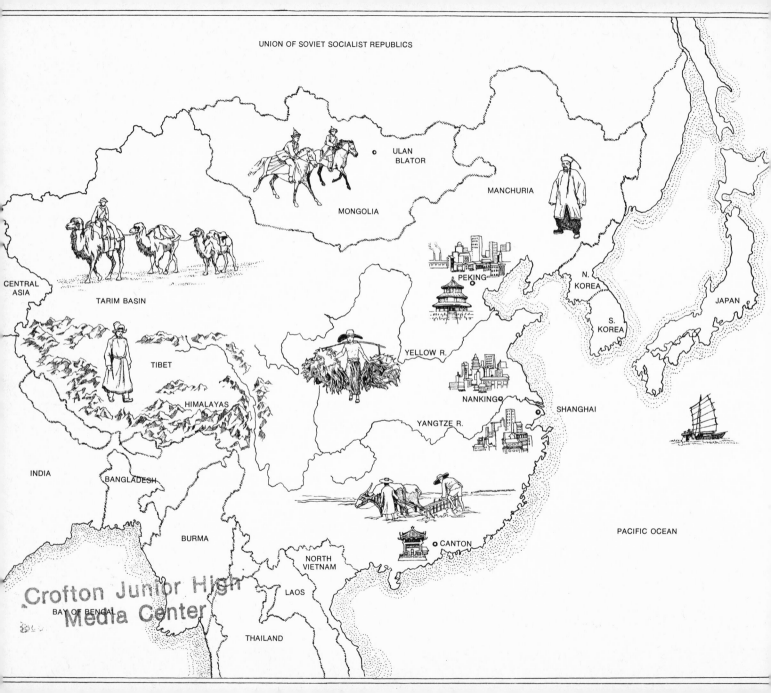

UNION OF SOVIET SOCIALIST REPUBLICS

ULAN
BLATOR

MONGOLIA

MANCHURIA

CENTRAL
ASIA

TARIM BASIN

PEKING

N.
KOREA

S.
KOREA

JAPAN

TIBET

YELLOW R.

HIMALAYAS

NANKING

SHANGHAI

YANGTZE R.

INDIA

BANGLADESH

BURMA

NORTH
VIETNAM

CANTON

PACIFIC OCEAN

LAOS

BAY OF BENGAL

THAILAND

CHINA

China is a country about the same size as the United States. One fourth of all the people in the world live there. They are, for the most part, farmers. With a five-thousand-year history, the longest continuous written history of any people in the world, the Chinese are credited with the invention of paper, printing, silk, porcelain, gunpowder, spaghetti and other things. They have beautiful sculpture, painting, architecture, furniture, costumes, and gardens.

China's neighbors are Russia to the north, Central Asia to the west, India to the southwest, Burma, Thailand, Laos, and Vietnam to the south, Korea to the northeast, and across the Yellow Sea, Japan. Because of this location, China has called herself "The Middle Kingdom," *Junggwo.*

Inside China there are four distinct geographical areas. In the northwest, desolate deserts and basins are the home of Turks who are nomads and herdsmen. For hundreds of years, camel caravans carried silk, spices, and teas to Europe across the desert and around the Tarim Basin. To the southwest lies Tibet, high in the Himalayas. Because West China is so mountainous and the climate is so extreme, only a tiny part of the population lives there.

Most of the population lives in East China. The Mandarin Chinese (or Han people, as they call themselves) are the largest ethnic group in China. They live in the northeast where the soil is rich. The mighty Yangtze and the Yellow River, called "China's Sorrow" because of the terrible floods, flow icy cold from the mountains in West China across the whole country and empty into the sea in the east. The main crop here is wheat. When Marco Polo visited the court of Genghis Khan, he ate the Chinese wheat noodle, and it was he who introduced into Italy this noodle which came to be known as spaghetti. The major cities of northeastern China are Peking, "the northern capital," and Shanghai, "on the sea."

Mongolia is slightly to the northwest of this part of China, and the capital city is Ulan Bator. China was conquered and ruled by foreign dynasties throughout her history, and a Mongol chieftain, Genghis Khan, who ruled almost all the known world in the thirteenth century, established the Yuan Dynasty in China.

Manchuria is further north still. The Manchus also established rule over China. They founded the Ching Dynasty. They made Chinese men wear pigtails as a symbol of subjugation.

South China is much warmer than North China, and the vegetation becomes increasingly tropical the further south one travels. The main cities of the South are Canton and Nanking, and the main crop is rice. Most Chinese-Americans originally came from Canton Province in South China.

China is a land of different peoples, customs, costumes, cuisines, and even different languages.

ITS LANGUAGES: CLASSICAL AND MODERN

Wen Yen

Wen yen is the ancient classical language of China. It was used only for writing and was never spoken. All books—poetry, history, drama, novels, religious texts—were written in classical Chinese. Scholar-gentlemen were trained to read the classics and to write poetry, and also to paint and to write beautifully. These skills were the foundation for the growth and development of the huge civil service which governed China for thousands of years.

All China had the same written language, *wen yen,* but there were hundreds of different spoken dialects. A dialect is a local language. Most of the people in the north spoke Mandarin, while the people in the south spoke Cantonese. People from Shanghai spoke Shanghai dialect. In some places in the south, the dialect changed every two or three miles. People in neighboring villages could not understand each other. To solve this problem, the government of the People's Republic of China made Mandarin the national language.

Bai Hwa

In the twentieth century, for the first time in China's long history, China has one language which is both written and spoken, and it is *bai hwa,* the language of the streets and countryside. Now everyone in China speaks the same dialect, which greatly improves communication and helps to unify the people. This is the same kind of language reform that Martin Luther, the German Reformation leader, made when he declared that the language of the people should be used in a church service, and not the classical Latin of the Church of Rome.

THE CHARACTER

In former times, even though the people spoke differently in different parts of China, they all read the same characters. The written word, the character, was the same for everyone. To understand the written Chinese word is to begin to understand a great deal about the Chinese people.

A Chinese word is called a character in English and a *dz* in Chinese. One thing that has remained constant in both literary and colloquial Chinese is the character, the basis of the whole Chinese language. The characters have been the same for thousands of years, beginning as crude drawings scratched in bone, then becoming the graceful lines drawn with the writing brush.

A Chinese character has three parts: sound, image, and meaning.

How It Appears to the Ear

Every Chinese character has a one-syllable pronunciation plus a tone, the note on which it is "sung." These tones give Chinese its sing-song quality.

Tones came about because Chinese has many words which sound alike. Sometimes, there are as many as fifty words which sound exactly the same. To tell these words apart, the Chinese invented tones, a kind of musical distinction made for the ear. The four tones in Mandarin Chinese are as follows:

The *First Tone* or *High Tone* is like a medium long buzz on a high, buzzing doorbell, or like the TI in do-re-mi-fa-so-la-TI-do.

The *Second Tone* or *Rising Tone* is the same sound your voice has when you answer the phone and say hel*lo*?

A serious old schoolmaster looks up from his book when he hears a light knock on the door. He says Ye-e-s? His voice dips down, then up again. This is the *Third Tone* or *Low Tone*.

The *Fourth Tone* or *Falling Tone* is your voice dropping at the end of the no in, "No! You can't feed the yak."

Take, for example, the word *tung*. This word, said in the four different tones, has four different meanings, and each meaning has a different written character.

First Tone (*High*)........*Tung*...to succeed   通

Second Tone (*Rising*)...*Tung*...together   同

Third Tone (*Low*).......*Tung*...to govern   統

Fourth Tone (*Falling*)....*Tung*...painful   痛

Thus, tones are used to tell spoken words apart which pronounce the same way.

How It Appears to the Eye

A character may consist of one image or a group of images. It communicates an idea. It is a certain way of looking at things which is special to the Chinese. For this reason, Chinese characters are sometimes called ideographs, or ''idea-writing.''

To appreciate this unique quality of the Chinese language, note the images in the following characters, and see how the whole is made up of the parts:

One Picture

Mouth

Three Pictures

A ''big mouth'' or border
A small mouth, or a person
A cowrie shell, or money

Two Pictures

Woman and Mouth

Four Pictures

A roof
One
A mouth
A field

14

In the next group of characters, note how images can be arranged in a variety of ways within a character to create visual beauty and balance:

One-picture Character 口

Mouth

Two-picture Characters

現

Now

星

Star

Three-picture Characters

Shau, a place name

活

Alive

然

Really

最

Very

Four-picture Characters

能

To be able

掛

To suspend

漫

Overflowing

戀

To be fond of

How It Appears to the Mind

The simplest way to make a word say what it means is to draw a picture of the thing: animal, plant, person, or object. Notice the images in ancient Chinese:

These are words which can be drawn. Some words, however, cannot be drawn. Numbers and directions, for example, are ideas and have no concrete image. Therefore, they cannot be drawn. Here are some symbols the Chinese created to express ideas:

Sun	⊖	Stone	石		One	一
Moon	𐄁	Hand	𡥃		Two	二
Woman	𡡞	Gate	門		Three	三
Water	川	Cart	車		Up	上
Eye	👁	Street	行		Down	下

Another way to convey meaning is to combine existing words and symbols to make new words, as follows:

Sun 日 and moon 月 together mean "bright." 明

Woman 女 and child 子 together mean "love." 好

Brain 田 and heart 心 together mean "think." 思

An eye 目 on two legs 儿 mean "to see." 見

Two men 从 on the ground 土 mean "to sit." 坐

Ten 十 mouths 口 mean "ten generations" or "ancient." 古

THE CHINESE SENTENCE

A Chinese sentence is made exactly the same way as an English sentence: first a noun, then a verb. These sentences are written across, left to right, Western-style, but they could also be written up and down, Chinese-style. In modern China, both styles are used.

我很好

Wo hen hua.
I am good

牛很大

Nyu hen da.
Cows are big.

我母親來

Wo muchin lai.
My mother is coming.

她吃飯

Ta chrfan.
She is eating.

我們説中國話

Women shwo junggwo hwa.
We speak Chinese.

你寫中國字

Ni sye junggwo dz.
You write Chinese characters.

我的朋友看書

Wode pengyou kanshu.
My friend is reading.

A Chinese noun is written the same way, whether it is singular or plural. *Ma* can mean horse or horses. 馬

Every Chinese noun has its own *measure*. In English we have only a few nouns with measures. We say, a *sheet* of paper, a *cup* of tea, a *bowl* of soup, a *pack* of wolves. But the Chinese give every noun a measure, or use one general measure which can go with any noun if the noun doesn't have a measure of its own. Because the measure is peculiar to the Chinese language, it cannot always be translated into English. Horse is a noun with its own measure—*shr.* 隻

The character for horse remains the same, whether singular or plural. *Shr,* the measure, remains the same. For all nouns that don't have a measure of their own, a general measure is used. This is 個 ,*ge*.

A measure is always used with a number for counting objects: yi*ge* (one thing); lyang*ge* (two things); san*ge* (three things).

Plain numbers: *yi, er, san, sz* (one, two, three, four) must be used for telephone numbers or for mathematics. (*Er* is the pure number two, *lyang* is two when counting objects).

One Horse
yi-shr-ma
Number-Measure-Noun

Five Horses
Wu-shr-ma
Number-Measure-Noun

On a scroll of Chinese writing, all the characters will be the same size, whether they have one stroke or twenty. The characters go down the page, in columns, and the columns go from right to left. The front of a Chinese book is where you would normally go to find the back.

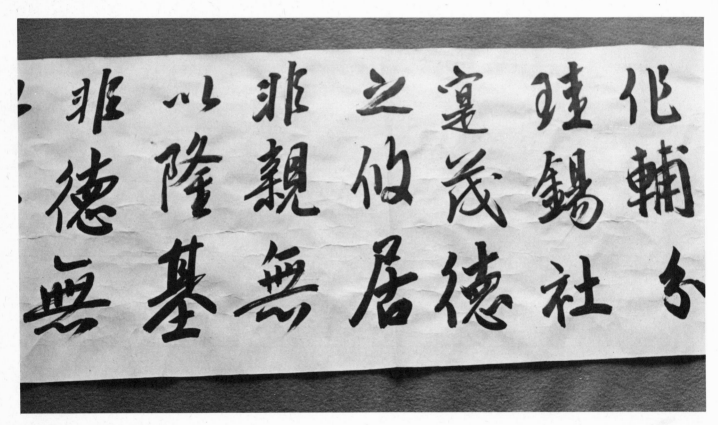

Calligraphy by C. C. Wang.

CALLIGRAPHY

Calligraphy is beautiful writing, and in China beautiful handwriting is considered a great art. Writing has always been important to the Chinese because it is the medium of preserving the culture and the wisdom of the sages. Calligraphy and culture are inseparable. Scholars, emperors, empresses, monks, nuns, generals, poets, and painters have prided themselves on their fine calligraphy. Although the Chinese were the first people to invent printing, they find the written word infinitely more beautiful than the printed word. No other script in the world has such beauty and variation of line.

Calligraphy is the art of writing characters. Characters have been scratched on tortoise shells and animal bones, carved in wood, cast on bronze vessels, and written with brush on silk and paper. Different writing materials give the characters a different look. The greatest styles are still copied and practiced by students and masters alike. Because the Chinese love beauty, they make each character pleasing to the eye. By putting many characters together, as in a poem or a quotation from the classics, the whole piece becomes a beautiful composition, a piece of art.

Chinese words make sense to the eye. Communication is achieved through meaning, but also through visual impact. The key to the art of calligraphy is form. The essence of calligraphy is movement, balance, flow, energy. Not the *meaning* of the character, but the *way* it is written is important.

Calligraphy is an art of lines, a celebration of the possibilities of lines. Different kinds of lines awake in us different sensations. The range of expression of the brush is almost limitless. Lines for the Chinese became the mirror of nature. They observed minutely all things in nature and tried to incorporate these shapes into the lines of writing to enrich it. As one famous calligrapher described it:

The characters may appear to be sitting or walking, flying or moving, going away or coming, sad or happy, like spring or summer, autumn or winter, like a bird pecking for food or an insect eating away wood, like a sharp knife or dagger or a strong bow and arrow, like water and fire, like trees and clouds, like the sun and moon following their course. Such is calligraphy.

The Strokes

To write English you use straight lines, curves, circles and dots.

To write characters, the Chinese use many different kinds of lines. The Chinese love nature and try to capture its activity in their writing. Their strokes look like bird claws, tiger paws, elephant's legs, a rhinoceros horn, phoenix-wing, dragon tail, dropping dew, suspended needle. The lines of Chinese writing are called strokes, and they must appear alive—sitting, walking or standing firmly.

For centuries there has been a scholarly controversy over just how many strokes there are in Chinese writing. Some calligraphers say seventy-two, some say thirty-four, but all agree they can be broken down into six basic strokes, as follows:

The Horizontal Stroke must look like clouds forming a thunderhead.

The Dots must look like rocks falling from a cliff with great force.

Sweeping Left Strokes look like a rhinoceros horn or a sharp sword.

Vertical Strokes must be like a thousand-year-old vine stem, still stout and strong.

Hooks get their name from the barbs at the end of the stroke.

Sweeping Right Strokes look like waves rolling up suddenly.

Because the strokes are basic to both calligraphy and painting, many painters have written about them in this way:

Long strokes will appear like a well-groomed scholar; short strokes, like a fiercely resolute disciple; lean strokes, like an emaciated resident of mountains and marshes; fat strokes, like a gentleman of leisure. Strong strokes will be like a soldier; graceful strokes like a beautiful woman; slanting strokes like a drunken deity, and upright strokes like a Confucian gentleman. . . .

Calligraphy may be compared to a dragon leaping, a tiger sleeping, playing in the surf, wandering in the sky, a beautiful woman, the sun setting or the moon rising. Thus, calligraphy and painting are indeed the same.

Painting and writing are first among the arts in China. Painting and writing were one and the same thing at one time: pictures. But each used pictures differently. Painting showed shapes accurately and in great detail, so that people could see things as they were. Writing was to transmit ideas, and detail was not important. Only the *idea* was important, so the picture became more and more simple. The strokes for calligraphy and painting are the same. In fact, calligraphy is abstract painting.

The master calligraphers tried to introduce as many variations as possible into their brush-strokes. In this they showed their skill and mastery. Students were instructed to copy the ancient models—all scripts and styles—for many years and, finally, if they had the inspiration, to develop a style of their own.

Calligraphy is compared to the dance, because the lines, like dancers, have rhythm, movement, and balance. Many calligraphers have been inspired by watching dancers or sword-fighters.

Calligraphy, like architecture, is an art of structures, a world of lines and shapes. Characters must stand squarely on the page. The upper and lower parts must balance. The left and right sides must fit together, neither too close nor too far apart. The sizes of the different elements must fit, very much like buildings, and only the length and width are left to the writer. A written character, like a photograph, can be made larger or smaller, but all the parts still must have the same relation to each other.

Even if some characters have only one stroke and others have twenty-four, or if some have only one picture and others have three, four, or five, all are composed within the frame of a square. Every new character is a fresh problem in structure, composition, and movement. The square is an aid to beginning writers. It helps them to arrange the elements correctly. In a single piece of calligraphy, every character—no matter how many strokes—will be written in the same size square in order to make the whole composition pleasing.

Tranquility and Spontaneity

The calligrapher's state of mind, when working, is tremendously important. Calligraphers must have complete detachment from outward disturbances. They need to cultivate a deep sense of tranquility, an emptiness of mind, a state of no-thought. They must work from the soul. This happens when the thoughts settle, when the mind is still.

The painter does not work in the rush of excitement. Although many calligraphers write fast, it is the stillness of mind which allows the inspiration to flow from the hand, brush, and ink onto the paper. To attain this freedom requires many years of patient disciplined study.

A classical book on Chinese calligraphy states:

> The artist must nourish in the heart gentleness and cheerfulness; the ideas must be harmonious. The heart should be quiet, honest, and sincere to the utmost, then the various aspects of human gladness and sorrow and of every other thing, be it pointed, oblique, bent or inclined, will appear naturally in the mind and be spontaneously brought out by the brush.

Calligraphy happens all in the moment. For this reason, it is said to be like the flow of life, ever-changing. It must be executed at once without hesitation, without thinking, without correction. One cannot go over a stroke because all corrections show when the ink dries. The brush must respond to the heart and mind of the calligrapher. So the mind must be still, and the brush technique must be perfect. The ideal is not to think nor to work at it. This is what takes the long years of practice: to use the brush as the extension of the spirit, without thinking.

As to looking at calligraphy and appreciating it, Shen Kua, a retired general, said in his *Dream Book:* "The wonderful parts of calligraphy and painting must be realized by the soul. . . . If one wishes to write, one must first release what is in the heart."

Often painters sit in meditation to still their thoughts and, beyond that, to tap the inner sources of inspiration. They value meditation because it develops the creative and intuitive faculties of the mind.

Calligraphy was always considered an important accomplishment by the emperors of China. It was impossible to enter the civil service if one did not have good calligraphy. One of the emperors of the Han Dynasty (c. 200 B.C.—200 A.D.) set up an official Academy of Calligraphy. During the previous dynasty, an overzealous emperor had burned all the classical books because the political ideas contained in them contradicted his own views of government. During the Han Dynasty, the classics were reconstructed from copies that had been hidden and saved. To preserve them, this Han emperor wished to have them engraved in stone. This enormous undertaking required many skilled calligraphers, so the emperor set up an academy. He arranged for students over seventeen to be tested for their talent in brush-writing. The candidates had to write 9,000 characters in the four major scripts. Those who showed promise went to the academy to begin training. Eventually they became court calligraphers.

Calligraphy was so highly prized that if a collector of paintings was known for his fine writing, he could write a poem or quotation on any painting in his collection and thus enhance its value.

Styles of Calligraphy

There are four basic styles of Chinese calligraphy. The *Seal Writing* is the most ancient and most similar to drawing. It also has the most pictorial detail. (All the ancient characters in this book are Seal Writing.) The *Official*

Script was used in the Han era for writing documents. It is a very even, legible, regular style, with round strokes and only slight variations in thickness and thinness of stroke.

The *Walking Script* has a faster rhythm and more movement than any of these styles. While the strokes within a character may run together, every character is distinct. The *Running Script* has the fastest rhythm and the most movement, and there are great differences in thickness and thinness of strokes. Sometimes, one cannot read the char-

acters because to the writer feeling and beauty of line are the most important features of this style. Thus, the styles of Chinese calligraphy range from the very still and pictorial to the very regular and legible, on through to the very free and abstract.

Within each style, every calligrapher's writing will be different. Some will be soft, some sharp; some will be bold, some graceful. The calligrapher strives to express his artistic sensitivity in the way he forms the stroke.

Handscroll: *Walking Style* calligraphy by C. C. Wang.

Seal Writing, the most ancient Chinese script, is closest to drawing. The lower right-hand character is a tree, while the upper left-hand character shows three hands above a tree.

Three examples of *Official Style*. The first is the softest. The strokes are very round on the ends and thinner in the middle. The second is sharper, with rounded even strokes. The third is the sharpest, with square even strokes.

Two examples of *Walking Style,* which is written faster than *Official Style.* The first is sharp and some strokes flow into one another, but each character is still very distinct. The second is very soft, has more movement, and all the strokes flow into one another.

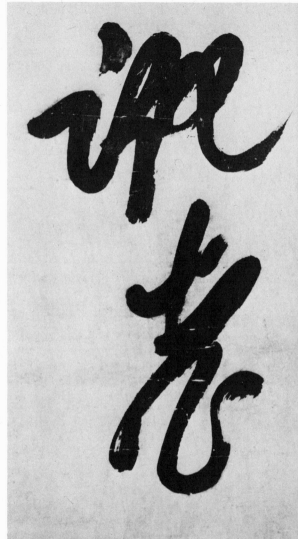

Running Style is the freest and has the most movement. Many strokes flow together. Even the characters flow together and some are not readable. This is pure movement, pure line, the expression of the calligrapher's mood and feeling.

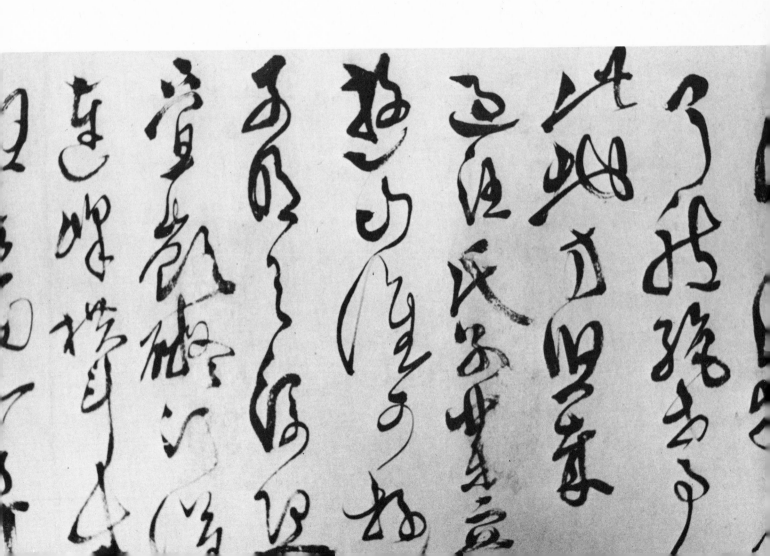

The Essence of Calligraphy

The major accomplishment of the calligrapher is brush-work. China's greatest calligrapher liked geese because the movement of their turning necks seemed to him like the movement of the wrist handling the brush. The movement of the wrist must be easy and unobstructed. Good brushwork means one must follow the rules, but be free and flexible in the movement so that everything seems to fly and move. What the Chinese like in their painting is the vibration of life. Another great calligrapher and poet, Po Chu-I, said that to express an idea or represent something properly, it must be turned over and over again in the mind until it unites with the soul.

The Four Treasures of the Calligrapher's Table

One of the nice things about calligraphy is the materials. The inkstone, inkstick, brush, and paper are called the Four Treasures of the Scholar's Table. Painters and calligraphers prize these treasures which can be had in the most precious materials, but they can also be bought inexpensively in art-supply stores.

The inkstone is used for grinding ink. At one end, there is a flat high place where the inkstick is ground with water; then it slants down to a well where the ink is collected. Inkstones have been made of stone, iron, copper, pottery, glass, oyster-shell, bamboo, wood, jade, even gold and silver.

The inkstick in China has been the most popular form of ink for 1,000 years. It is ground with water on the inkstone to make ink of whatever blackness is desired. Often the inksticks are beautifully decorated with gold characters. These, too, are highly prized. There is a story about a scholar of the Sung Dynasty who had an inkstick made by a famous ink-maker. It was thin as a chopstick and less than a foot long. The scholar and his brother used the inkstick for over ten years, writing more than 500 characters a day.

The ink is made by mixing soot and glue. The soot comes from burning pine or fir wood in a kiln, or by burning vegetable oils in a clay bowl. The black residue is then mixed with glue made from hides of deer, cow, donkey, and other animals, or fish skin. The soot must be shiny and black; the glue must be clear and clean. The mixture is then molded and dried into a cake. When rubbed in a little water, the stick makes liquid ink.

The Chinese use rice paper for writing. It is very absorbent and provides a stark contrast to the blackness of ink. The rice paper "takes" the ink and lets it spread. Paper was used in China 1,000 years before it was used in Europe; before that, the Chinese wrote on silk.

The Chinese brush has a hollow bamboo handle and a finely pointed tip of animal hair. For writing the point is still and only the tip is used. It is a versatile writing instrument because of the wonderful variety of lines it can produce. A brush with stray or broken hairs must never be used because the hairs will leave little lines of ink. This would spoil the effect of the characters. Brush-stems are mostly bamboo, but sometimes they are made of gold, silver, ivory, jade, crystal, tortoise-shell, rhinoceros horn, porcelain, and sandalwood. A great variety of hairs have been used to make brushes, among them rabbit, fox, wolf, mouse whiskers, goat, sable, deer, hare, and sometimes even children's hair.

Many calligraphers and painters made their own brushes. Brushmaking itself was a very exalted profession because art was held in such high esteem. There are tales of brushmakers who departed to the heavens astride a piece of rainbow-colored cloud in a blaze of dazzling light. Others were said to have turned themselves into exotic birds that eternally soared in the heavens.

Close-up of inkstone.

This Inkstone, about 300 years old, is carved with moon, clouds, sheep, and water. It is made from special stone which comes from Canton. The stone is smooth for easy grinding, so that the ink will not be grainy and rough. Makers of inkstones, inksticks, brushes, and paper were considered artists.

Left
This 100-year-old inkstick is made from pine soot which has a blue-black color and a very fine-grained consistency. The liquid ink is poured into a mold. When it hardens, the mold is broken, and the inkstick will have the design of the mold on it.

Right
Various writing brushes. The brush-holder, made of the most valuable teakwood, is only used for precious objects and is extremely heavy.

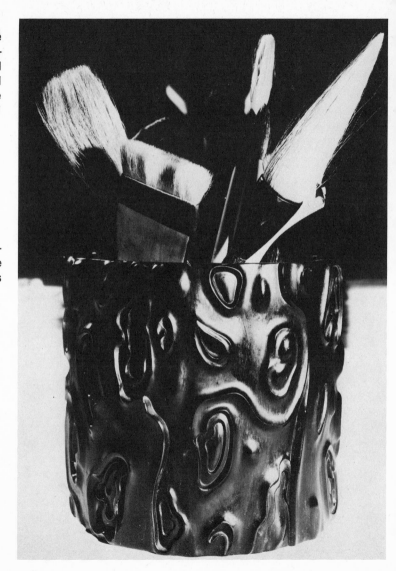

HOW TO WRITE CHARACTERS

The Brush
How to hold the brush is the first step. The brush is held perpendicularly, with the thumb on the left side of the handle and the index finger on the right side, an inch above the thumb. The third finger should be in front of the brush and the fourth finger behind it. The fingers should be firm, the palm hollow. The brush must be supported on all four sides. No one should be able to snatch it out of your hand. This position allows you to dip, twist, and turn the brush in any direction.

Only the tip of the brush is used for writing. If you are using the brush for the first time, it will be a bit stiff. Let it stay in warm water for half an hour before you begin.

Practice holding the brush properly. Stand the brush up on its very tip to get the feel of it. Then, dip only the tip into the ink. You can use Pelikan drawing ink, or any commercial black India ink. Now you are ready to begin. To make thin strokes, stand the brush up on its very tip. Press down to make the strokes thicker.

The correct way to hold the brush.

33

The Paper

Spread out a sheet of paper. Rice paper is best because it absorbs the ink and lets it dry immediately. Rice paper is also desirable because it is translucent. You can see through it, to the nine-fold square. You can buy rice paper in sheets or rolls. Any other translucent paper will also do. All supplies can be bought at any art supply store.

The Nine-fold Square

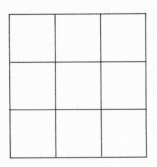

Chinese children practice the strokes until they can write them well. They write simple characters first. They start with a medium-sized brush and make ten medium-sized characters (approximately three inches square) each day. This size is easiest to write. Later, when they can handle a smaller brush, they add ten small characters.

To help compose and balance the character, it used to be written in a square. Then, to make composition easier, an anonymous calligrapher invented the nine-fold square, a square which is divided into nine parts.

This device helps one to place and balance all parts of a character well. You will find a sheet of nine-fold squares at the back of this book for your use in practicing calligraphy. If you wish, you can make your own nine-fold squares, using graph paper. Mark the square with a magic marker or any felt-tip pen, so you can see it.

Place your sheet of writing paper over the nine-fold square. Practice placing the parts of each character, so that the character is perfectly balanced in the square. Each character should seem to be standing strongly on its own "feet."

The Stroke and Stroke Order

The second step is to learn the six basic strokes. These appear on page 22 and are repeated here in horizontal form for your convenience. The strokes should be practiced over and over again, until you can make them well. Pay special attention to the thick parts (pressing down on the brush) and the thin parts (using the tip of the brush), and also to the direction of the stroke. Then, when you write the characters, every stroke will be beautiful.

The order for putting the strokes together to form a character is called stroke order. Correct stroke order is essential for calligraphy, and for looking up words in the Chinese dictionary where words are listed by stroke order and by the number of strokes. There are seven principles for the order in which the strokes should be written. The rules are as follows:

Keep in mind that all characters occupy a square:
1. Always go from upper left-hand corner to lower right.
2. Always go from left to right.
3. Always go from top to bottom.
4. Write the outside part first, then the inside.
5. Write horizontal lines first, then vertical lines.
6. Write slanting left strokes first, then slanting right strokes.
7. Write the center stroke first, the left stroke next, then the right.

The stroke order is natural to this kind of writing. It will become more and more familiar to you as you practice. However, do not try to memorize the stroke order if it prevents you from going on with your practice. Just practice.

DICTIONARY FOR PRACTICE

How the Character Has Changed
The peoples of the world write their languages down in one of two different ways: alphabets or pictures. English is an alphabet language. Alphabets are used to write the sound of a word. They usually have one symbol for every sound. An alphabet word makes sense to your ear. A picture language makes sense to your eye. Chinese is a picture language. It has one picture for every word. Sometimes, this one picture will be made up of a number of smaller pictures put together.

Picture-words can be made in several ways. The simplest way is to draw the animal, plant, person, or object. When a word stood for an abstract idea, like a number or a direction, which cannot be drawn easily, a symbol was made up. The words in this dictionary are both drawings and symbols.

The basic idea of Chinese picture-words has stayed the same for thousands of years. But when the writing-brush came into use, the words acquired a new appearance. The most ancient style of writing was rounder and had more detail. With the brush, the writing became squarer and had very little detail (more abstract, more artistic). The examples in the chart below illustrate this change:

	Ancient	Modern
Sun	日	日
Moon	月	月
Woman	女	女
Water	水	水
Eye	目	目
Stone	石	石
Hand	手	手
Gate	門	門
Cart	車	車
Street	行	行

Sometimes it is easier to see the original meaning of a Chinese word in the older, more detailed form. The modern word then makes more sense. In this dictionary, the ancient character is given when it helps the reader to understand how the modern word came to be.

Here, then, is your dictionary for practice. The characters chosen are simple everyday words which are easy to understand and easy to write. The character is given, along with its meaning and its pronunciation. The stroke order for each character is included to show how to write the word, step by step. Just follow along, adding a stroke at a time, until you have the whole character.

MAN
(REN)

This word is a drawing of a man walking.

Stroke Order: ノ 人

BIG
(DA)

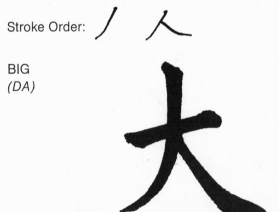

Man with an additional stroke, indicating outstretched arms, suggests the quality of bigness.

Stroke Order: 一 ナ 大

HEAVEN
(TYAN)

Man with two strokes added shows a big man whose head touches the sky.

Stroke Order: 一 二 于 天

WATER
(SHWEI)

The ancient word for water is 川, a drawing of a stream with banks on either side.

Stroke Order:] 才 水 水

WOMAN
(NYU)

The above word is the modern version of 女

Stroke Order: く 女 女

RAIN
(YU)

The ancient word for rain is a cloud with drops of water falling. 雨

Stroke Order:

一 冂 冂 币 雨 雨 雨 雨

EARTH
(TU)

This character is a simple version of the ancient word , a drawing of an altar of the soil. China has always been an agricultural society and in ancient times, altars were built to ensure good crops and fertility of the land.

Stroke Order: 一 十 土

FIRE
(HWO)

The ancient drawing was which shows the jumping quality of fire.

Stroke Order: 丶 丷 少 火

TREE
(MU)

In this drawing of a tree, the vertical stroke represents the trunk, the horizontal stroke represents branches, and the sweeping strokes stand for roots.

 Two trees together is the word for forest.

Three trees together means thicket.

Stroke Order: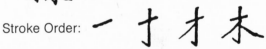

MOUNTAIN
(SHAN)

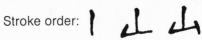

The modern version of the ancient drawing of mountains.

Stroke order: 丨 山 山

SUN
(R)

The old drawing was ⊖, a good example of how Chinese was round in the ancient writing and became square.

Stroke Order: 丨 冂 日 日

MOON
(YWE)

The original drawing was a crescent moon, ⊅

Stroke Order: 丿 冂 月 月

HORSE
(MA)

A very good drawing of a horse. Broken down, 𠃌 is the neck with the mane flying, ⁊ is the back and tail, 灬 are the four legs.

Stroke Order: 一 厂 F F 馬 馬 馬 馬 馬 馬

SHEEP
(YANG)

羊

A picture of a sheep's face and his big horns, an adaptation of the ancient word

Stroke Order: 、 ⺊ ⺊ ⺊ ⺼ ⺼ 羊

COW
(NYU)

牛

A picture of the cow's face and horns

Stroke Order: ノ ⺊ ⺊ 牛

HOUSE
(JYA)

家

The character for house is a drawing of a pig  under a roof ⼧, an image natural to an agricultural society.

Stroke Order: 、 ⺍ ⼧ 宀 宀

宁 家 家 家 家

Symbols

UP, ABOVE
(SHANG)

The concept of "upness" is illustrated by one line above another line.

Stroke Order: 丨 卜 上

DOWN, BELOW
(SYA)

The concept of "downness" is represented by one small line below another line.

Stroke Order: 一 丁 下

CENTER
(JUNG)

Above is the modern version of the ancient symbol for center, an arrow in the center of a target.

Stroke Order: 丨 口 口 中

Pronouns

Singular Pronouns.

I or ME
(WO)

Stroke Order:

丿 二 千 千 我 我 我

YOU
(NI)

Stroke Order:

丿 亻 亻 你 你 你 你

HE, SHE or HIM, HER
(TA)

Stroke Order:

丿 亻 亻 他 他

For the plural, simply add *men* to the singular pronoun.

WE, US
(WOMEN)

我們

Stroke Order for *MEN:*

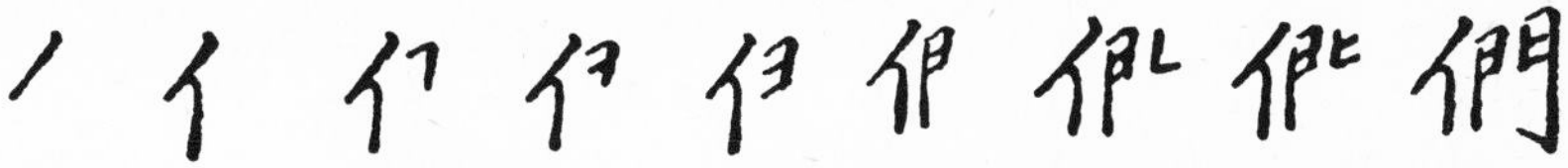

ノ 亻 亻ヿ 亻ヿ 亻ヨ 們 們 們 們

YOU
(NIMEN)

你們

THEY, THEM
(TAMEN)

他們

Following are the characters used for arithmetic, counting, and telephone numbers, and also for the months. The name of the month consists of a number, plus the character for moon. Thus January is one-moon, February is two-moons, and so on.

Number

Month

一	One	*Yi*	一月	January	*Yi-Ywe*
二	Two	*Er*	二月	February	*Er-Ywe*
三	Three	*San*	三月	March	*San-Ywe*
四	Four	*Sz*	四月	April	*Sz-Ywe*
五	Five	*Wu*	五月	May	*Wu-Ywe*
六	Six	*Lyou*	六月	June	*Lyou-Ywe*

Number

七	Seven	*Chi*
八	Eight	*Ba*
九	Nine	*Jyou*
十	Ten	*Shr*
十一	Eleven	*Shr-Yi*
十二	Twelve	*Shr-Er*

Month

七月	July	*Chi-Ywe*
八月	August	*Ba-Ywe*
九月	September	*Jyou-Ywe*
十月	October	*Shr-Ywe*
十一月	November	*Shr-Yi-Ywe*
十二月	December	*Shr-Er-Ywe*

Other Sources

Calligraphy: Yee, Chiang. *Chinese Calligraphy.* Cambridge: Harvard University Press, Rev. Ed., 1973.

Language: Wolff, Diane. *An Easy Guide to Everyday Chinese.* New York: Harper & Row, 1974.

Painting: Sze, Mai-Mai. *The Way of Chinese Painting.* New York: Random House Vintage Book, 1959.

Bibliography

Chen, Chih-Mai. *Chinese Calligraphers and Their Art.* New York: Cambridge University Press, 1966.

Driscoll, Lucy, and Toda, Kenji. *Chinese Calligraphy.* Chicago: University of Chicago Press, 1935.

Ecke, Tseng Yu-ho. *Chinese Calligraphy.* Philadelphia and Boston: Philadelphia Museum of Art, and Boston Book and Art Publisher, 1971.

Illustrated Atlas of China. Rand McNally, 1972.

Siren, Osvald. *The Chinese on the Art of Painting.* New York: Schocken Books, 1963.

Nine-fold Square
for Practice

About the Author
Diane Wolff is a New York writer and a specialist on Chinese art and calligraphy. She studied at Briarcliff College and at Columbia University. This is her second book on the Chinese language.

About the Book
The text was set in Linotype Helvetica. The book is illustrated with original calligraphy and photographs.

495.1 Wolff, Diane 00 995
WOL   Chinese writing